W9-API-185

THE AMERICAN DREAM?

Shing Yin Khor is an Ignatz-winning cartoonist and installation artist who is exploring personal narrative, new human rituals, and collaborative worldbuilding through graphic memoir, science fiction, and large-scale art structures. As a cartoonist, their work has been published in *The Toast*, *The Nib*, *Catapult*, *Huffington Post*, and *Bitch* magazine. They make the road-trip adventure comic Tiny Adventure Journal and the tender queer science fiction comic Center for Otherworld Science. Shing lives in Los Angeles.

Zest Books™
An imprint of Lerner Publishing Group, Inc.
241 First Avenue North
Minneapolis, MN 55401 USA

For reading levels and more information, look up this title at www.lernerbooks.com. Visit us at zestbooks.net.

Main body text set in Dirty Mermaid.

Library of Congress Cataloging-in-Publication Data

Names: Khor, Shing Yin, author.
Title: The American dream? : a journey on Route 66 discovering dinosaur statues, muffler men, and the perfect breakfast burrito / by Shing Yin Khor.
Description: Minneapolis : Zest Books, [2019] | Audience: Ages: 11–18. | Audience: Grades: 9–12. |
Identifiers: LCCN 2018060700 (print) | LCCN 2019003990 (ebook) | ISBN 9781541578531 (eb pdf) | ISBN 9781541578524 (lb : alk. paper) | ISBN 9781942186373 (pb : alk. paper)
Subjects: LCSH: Khor, Shing Yin—Travel—Comic books, strips, etc.—Juvenile literature. | United States Highway 66—Description and travel—Comic books, strips, etc.—Juvenile literature. | Asian American women—Travel—Comic books, strips, etc.—Juvenile literature. | Immigrants—United States—Biography—Comic books, strips, etc.—Juvenile literature. | Asian American women artists—Biography—Comic books, strips, etc.—Juvenile literature.
Classification: LCC F595.3 (ebook) | LCC F595.3 .K46 2019 (print) | DDC 917.804/34—dc23

LC record available at https://lccn.loc.gov/2018060700

Manufactured in the United States of America
1-46974-47843-1/9/2019

THE AMERICAN DREAM?

A JOURNEY ON ROUTE 66

Discovering DINOSAUR STATUES, MUFFLER MEN, and the PERFECT BREAKFAST BURRITO

A Graphic Memoir by **SHING YIN KHOR**

WITHDRAWN

Z ZEST BOOKS
MINNEAPOLIS

For Jason

66 Motel sign.
Needles, CA.

The second America was one I first encountered in the Grapes of Wrath.

primary school prefect uniform. I was kind of a nerd.

book!

The story of the Joad family making their way west, past deserts and barren expanses of land, in search of the American Dream.

ORANGE PICKERS WANTED

It was an incredible journey, filled with dusty roads and big hopes.

It is a story that has stuck with me for decades, that feeling of desperately searching for something better, for a new start.

I can't help but relate to that, as an immigrant and artist.

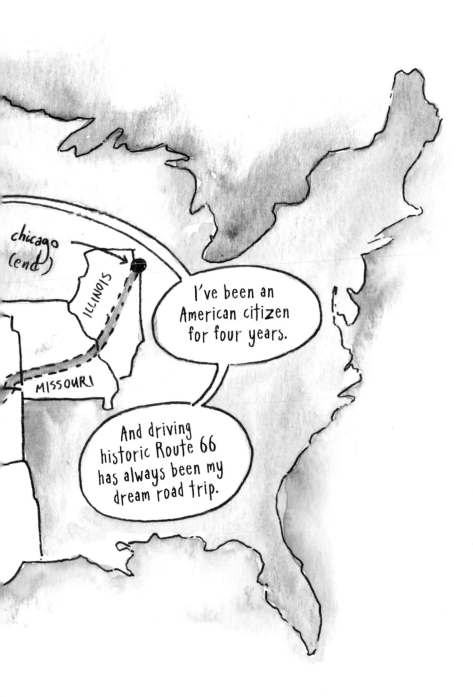

For me, this is a pilgrimage.

The concept of the American Dream is something that I've long struggled with.

I understand the modern immigrant interpretation, the one where we work hard, get the right visas, and eventually get to stand in a large room as newly minted American citizens watching terrible patriotic videos.

DID you KNOW?

At the naturalization ceremony, many new Americans are subjected to an awful, and awfully patriotic song.

...but at least I know I'm freeee...

AUGH.

But this westward trail is still more foreign to me. I've lived in my Los Angeles bubble for over a decade, but I'm not sure I'll feel really American until I see more of America.

Fig A.
Basic Adventure Gear!

adventure hat

messy hair →

← favorite jacket

well-used leather satchel

beaten-up camera →

large water bottle ↗

tiny adventure dog! ↓

comfy pants with lots of pockets

shoes for → lots of walking

MY CAMPING ESSENTIALS...

very warm
down sleeping bag

adorable
tiny lantern

tent
stakes

tent

first
aid kit

knife

tiny
camp
stove

snacks!

water!

Our budget is small, so we'll be spending a lot
of time camping, but I'm not exactly roughing it.

portable
speaker

thermos

book!

favorite
camp mug

This is
really nice,
I swear.

The actual historical start (or end) of Route 66 in California is the intersection of Lincoln and Olympic. There is a sign at the Santa Monica Pier, which is prettier. Here, there is just a dentist's office.

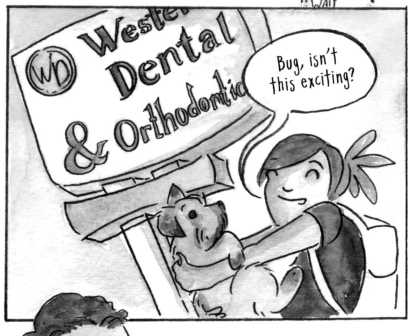

(a bad pun interlude, from my friend Scott)

The original Route 66 never extended to this sign at the Santa Monica Picr, but it is still a nice view.

SANTA MONICA

66

End of the Trail

Burgers Fries

There isn't much to mark Route 66 in Los Angeles. The first time I see a sign is in Hollywood, and it would have been easy to miss in the bustle of the city.

ugh traffic whyyy

Actually, I spend my first three hours of driving Route 66 in traffic.

AUGH.

I decide to stop for the night near Barstow. I'm traveling on a tiny budget, so I consider the two closest campgrounds.

One is named Sawtooth Canyon.
The other is named Owl Canyon.

I decide to go with the owls.

I'm trying out my car camping setup for the first time. Which is to say, I'm just trying to sleep in my car.

My car is a 2010 Honda Fit, with the back seats folded down.

easily accessible backpack

Bug's food and water

A comfy pillow is important.

sleeping pad and blankets

Bug's crate and pillows

Most things I have are stored in plastic bins.

It's working out well, although I wouldn't recommend it for anyone taller than 4'6", and I am 5'0".

The campsite is nearly empty.

Bug and I clamber up a ridge to watch the sunset. It always amazes me that just a few hours away from Los Angeles, the night sky is clear and the stars insistently visible.

In the morning, I take a long walk to the least appealing building at a campground.

Vault toilets are essentially giant holes in the ground filled with poop.

But you get walls!

(They are actually pretty nice, for being giant poop vaults.)

On the way back, I run into two friendly rangers, Arthur and Miguel. Arthur grew up in East Los Angeles, but he loves the desert.

The desert season is just starting, and soon the hills will be in bloom. It's beautiful!

They send me off to the Bureau of Land Management field office in Barstow, where they tell me I can learn a lot about their Route 66 restoration work.

They also care a lot about desert tortoises.

He gets lost in bureaucratic talk for a bit but lights up when I ask him why Route 66 is still appealing to travelers.

There's just something about the mystique and nostalgia of Route 66. It was the Main Street of America! You know Steinbeck called it the Mother Road?

There's something legendary about this road that still draws people in...millions of people come to see this history.

Route 66 maps

lots of brochures

so much paper

even more paper

a binder full of the Route 66 revitalization plan

a backup of everything on CD

There is a stretch of road between Newberry Springs and Ludlow that is a teeth-chattering combination of potholes and patches.

It runs entirely parallel to I-40, where smooth asphalt mocks me as I wonder if this road is going to rattle my tiny car apart.

It would be much easier to take the highway.

ROY'S
VACANCY
MOTEL
CAFE

Amboy, CA

33

Fortunately, a good way to make sure I finish a project is to make it difficult.

a BRIEF HISTORY of ROUTE 66

1926

Route 66 begins as a loose collection of roads which link mostly rural communities. It is designated in 1926.

the start of the Great Depression

1929

Many families travel Route 66 during the Great Depression to seek a new life in the West.

1930s

35

1940s

During World War II, Route 66 becomes a primary transport corridor, connecting several new military installations and bringing job seekers to the West Coast.

More than 2000 miles all the way... get your kicks, on Route 66...

Nat King Cole records "(Get Your Kicks on) Route 66."

The song is a hit and resonates with motorists all over the country seeking to explore America after the war.

1946

1950s

The increase in tourism leads to a rise in motels, diners, and tacky tourist attractions...for a little while, at least.

Mr. D'z
ROUTE 66 DINER

Kingman, AZ

ROUTE
INTERSTATE
40

Newer and more modern highways begin to bypass Route 66.

By the 1970s, most of the road has been replaced.

Route 66 is officially removed from the highway system in 1985.

BUG
at
JACKRABBIT
TRADING POST
Joseph City, AZ

not actually
the world's
largest statue
of a jackrabbit,
somehow

Arizona greets me with the most charming mountain pass landscapes and wild donkeys.

Wild donkey. Bug is not very happy about its presence.

OATMAN, AZ

Oatman is an old mining town that has reinvented itself many times and now is entirely a cheesy but charming Route 66 tourist attraction.

1900s

Oatman was only a gold mining town for about ten years!

Gregory Peck ↓

1960s

Debbie Reynolds →

Several Hollywood films were shot in Oatman, including *How the West Was Won*.

After we drive through the mountain pass, Kingman delivers on its promise of vintage American kitsch. It is a perfectly curated blend of intentionally placed trains and diners, and, if you wander, abandoned motels and garages that used to serve Route 66 traffic.

The Powerhouse Visitor Center used to be an electrical substation. It is a Route 66 museum now.

Kingman's motto is "The Heart of Historic Route 66."

After Kingman, the landscape changes to the raggedy discards of an American dream.

SAKE PIC

KODAK FILM

UCE   U.S. POST OFFICE

The Arizona stretch of Route 66 is littered with them, these shells of tourist traps and tiny towns, all within feet of the asphalt. I try not to get too maudlin about it, but the cycle of human occupation is endlessly fascinating to me, and the dry desert heat of Arizona has preserved these places well.

At Two Guns, an abandoned former campground and tourist attraction, I run into a biker, Bruce, and we explore the town together.

I retired a few years ago! Figured I could buy a bike and explore America, or be a Zen Buddhist.

You could do both?

Hmm. Yeah.

49

TWO GUNS

Two Guns is the site of a major Apache genocide in 1878, where 42 Apaches were suffocated in a cave.

The site became a trading post in 1922, most notably by Harry "Indian" Miller, who turned the cave into a tourist trap called the "Apache Death Cave." He also built a zoo.

Then Harry Miller murdered one of his landlords in an argument.

He was then attacked by his mountain lion, lynx, and Gila monster, and also had a slew of legal troubles.

Eventually, taking the hint, he left Two Guns in 1930.

Two Guns went on to live a varied life as a campground and rest stop, although the entire town caught fire in 1971. The last caretaker of the place died in 2000; the place is now abandoned.

I can't say I put much stock in curses, but Two Guns is not a lucky town.

Indistinct shapes dance in my periphery and are never there when I look. I'm glad Bruce is here, because if there is a vengeful prowling beast of cursed souls past hanging around, he might get eaten first.

Meteor City Trading Post claims to have the world's largest dream catcher.

Meteor City Trading Post is more recently abandoned. I've been here before, so I recommend it to Bruce.

It used to be one of many Trading posts on southwestern Route 66 that sold trinkets like cactus candy, petrified wood, and made-in-China dream catchers.

Now, most of them are gone.

There is a snowy owl in there!

OOH!

I've been meeting a lot of interesting people on Route 66.

Route 66 is a common route for bikers like Bruce. They are probably the ones following the truest route and all the little unmaintained roads. In the summer, it is common to see a row of Harleys parked outside the Roadkill Cafe or any other diner.

OPEN

BREAKFAST

Roadkill Cafe
Seligman, AZ

The route is also common among RVers, who are usually very nice. They are often retired older couples or families with good dogs.

And then there are the tour buses. They are large and air-conditioned and filled with people who really enjoy crowding around the Route 66 painted road markers for pictures.
Which is cute, except that this is an active road, and they are standing in the middle of it.

You have to be kidding me, right?

It is pretty annoying, but I am not comfortable with the false distinction between tourist and traveler.

While I'm busy being excited about decay and deliberately overthinking the nature of tourism, Arizona is busy preserving its Route 66 history. Seligman, AZ, has an especially enthusiastic embrace of Route 66 kitsch.

The popularity of Disney's *Cars* has also resulted in some adaptation to that cartoonish aesthetic...

Snow Cap Drive-in
Seligman, AZ

...the effect is actually slightly ghoulish.

I stop by the Snow Cap for lunch, where they still dish out jokes in the tradition of Juan Delgadillo, whom many give credit for the revitalization of Route 66 tourism in Arizona.

Juan Delgadillo died in 2004 but his humor lives on, over a decade later.

A burger and a small root beer float, please!

One SMALL root beer!

→ tiny cup

The staff also tosses rubber chickens around.

Delgadillo covered this 1936 Chevy in all sorts of kitschy baubles to attract visitors to the Snow Cap.

SHAKES

DELLA SNO

The burger is perfectly serviceable, but as I sit outside and watch tourists wander by, it feels like a particularly American sort of burger.

Royce and Nita pile up every soft thing in their house for me to sleep on.

It is the absolute best little blanket nest in the world.

Nita's an educator. Royce calls her "Pie," as in:

Royce is an artist and metalworker. Nita calls him "Pi," as in: π a statue in front of Rainbow Rock Shop in Holbrook

a kind of janky statue at Stewart's Petrified Wood in Holbrook

poor mannequin

take me back to DINOSAUR CITY

HOLBROOK, AZ

One of my favorite things about Arizona is the panoply of roadside dinosaur statues!

Some are handmade.

GRAND CANYON CAVERNS!

Peach Springs, AZ

The statues are almost all inaccurate, and
most of these dinosaurs were definitely
not discovered in Arizona.

I'm still a total sucker for their ridiculousness.

My friend Matt is a paleontologist at the Petrified Forest National Park and happy to educate me.

Coelophysis and Chindesaurus are the only two dinosaurs to have been discovered at the Petrified Forest.

CHINDESAURUS

A small bipedal carnivore from the late Triassic period.

The name means "ghost lizard."

COELOPHYSIS

A very small and fast runner, also from the late Triassic. A fairly common specimen to find.

Taman Botanikal Melaka
Malacca, Malaysia

I grew up in the colonial-era port city of Malacca, Malaysia, which is a bit of a tourist town.

MALAYSIA

also Malaysia

Malacca

After school, while waiting for the bus, I used to play in the ruins of a 14th-century Portuguese fort because it was down the street from the Catholic convent I attended.

It is quite possible that the horrors of colonialism are a bit opaque to a ten-year-old.

KILL THEM ALL!

It is both oddly privileged and quite uncomfortable to grow up in a city surrounded by so much marketable culture.

It often felt like the mere act of being a local near a tourist attraction was to be a performer in someone else's narrative.

OK! SMILE! GOOD! OK!

can speak English and is also not hard of hearing

This fort, A Famosa, has been occupied by the Portuguese, Dutch, and British.

Blue Mesa,
Petrified Forest National Park

Bug is a Petrified Forest National Park Junior Ranger. She has a badge, so it must be true.

JUNIOR PARK RANGER

petrified wood log

I already love New Mexico.

For me, it is the perfect blend of kitschy Americana, with a strong helping of Native American art and just enough city.

It's also where I've heard one of the best sentences ever said to me: "Would you like green or red chile?"

the abandoned Mountain Lodge motel
Albuquerque, NM

(The correct answer is "Christmas!")

green chile sauce

cheese

Red

Green

egg

potatoes

red chile sauce

bacon

New
Mexico

the BREAKFAST BURRITO

My artist friends Brandt and Kathie live in Albuquerque and I've visited them a few times. They run an art gallery on Central Avenue, which is part of historic Route 66, and they have a very comfortable couch.

I didn't think I was that much of a city girl until this drive. But I am acutely aware that I haven't had any sushi in weeks and I've been cycling through the same three pairs of socks and underwear.

...zzzzzzzzzz...

All of my deep conversations have been with a scruffy dog.

She is, however, a very good listener.

Motel signs in Albuquerque

I drive on, choosing to drive the early route instead of the later 1950s alignment toward Santa Fe.

A Spanish mission built in Isleta Pueblo. Most of the town's population are part of the Southern Tiwa tribe.

An abandoned adobe house. Eventually, the outer adobe covering falls away, leaving piles of bricks.

American owned. AMERICAN owned. It might not mean anything to most people, but as a brown American, I know exactly what that means. The term "Patel Motel" is used as a pejorative, a play on the term "no-tell motel," but with an extra helping of racism.

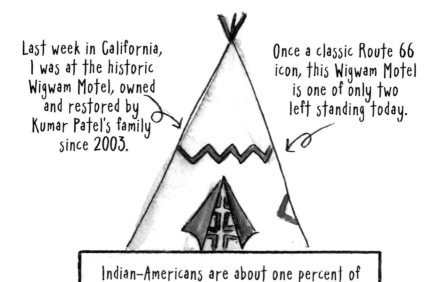

Last week in California, I was at the historic Wigwam Motel, owned and restored by Kumar Patel's family since 2003.

Once a classic Route 66 icon, this Wigwam Motel is one of only two left standing today.

Indian-Americans are about one percent of the United States population, but they own approximately half of the motels in America.

Did you love Route 66 before you bought this motel?

ROUT 66

We didn't know about it then, but we care about it now. It's a good thing.

← postcards!

I wish I could adequately express my anger.
For now, I'll drive on.

I can only find one radio station here, and it is playing Jesus Rock, which gives me youth group flashbacks. The religion here itches under my skin and makes me feel especially out of place.

I was raised in and with a variety of religions and even spent some time in the embrace of a chosen church community. I shouldn't feel that awkward.

After the constant flatness, it is nice to drive into Amarillo, the only city on the Texas stretch of Route 66.

BLUE SKY
Asian Market

huh.

And here, I am surprised.

I was definitely expecting more cowboy hats, I think.

It turns out that Amarillo is a major refugee relocation center. Many refugees, from decades of wars and periods of civil unrest, have settled in middle-of-nowhere Texas.

myanmar

somalia

Iraq

Vietnam

syria

I'm eating fishballs for breakfast in Texas!

As the new kid in school, Christianity was an easy way of belonging, and I wanted to belong. I could simply attend youth group, and people would stop telling me they would pray for me.

My path to nonbelief was less exact. I saw more shooting stars. I stopped asking them questions.

I stopped expecting common natural phenomena to serve as divine guidance.

I found different ways to fit in. I fell in love with other dead old men.

I just moved on, like shedding a costume that always fit a little bit oddly.

I expected to be lonely on this drive, but until Texas, I didn't expect that I would feel so foreign and displaced and set apart from the communities I would be driving through. I feel different here.

CADILLAC RANCH

I am the first in my family to pursue art as a career, which is confusing to many of my relatives. Being at the Cadillac Ranch reassures me that I am probably on the right path.

The Cadillac Ranch is a balm for my awkward melancholy. There are visitors here, the most people I have seen since leaving New Mexico. It is a comfort that there is a place for outsider art in this world. I am happy that there are places for honest art and art that tells stories, for art that doesn't have a clear purpose yet but to exist.

Cadillac Ranch
Amarillo, TX

Cowboy Motel Sign
Amarillo, TX

Oklahoma declares that it is "Native America" on its license plates, and I drive through several reservations in the state.

OKLAHOMA APR
RT66
NATIVE AMERICA

Inspired by Native American art, this is the largest concrete totem pole in America.

Ed Galloway's TOTEM POLE PARK

SPEED LIMIT 6

Foyil, OK

Driving Route 66 has shown me more of Native American culture than any of my education has, even if it is steeped in the unabashed tourist courting of concrete teepees and dream-catcher-hawking gift shops that line the route.

WELCOME TO
OKLAHOMA
NATIVE AMERICA

I ask my friend Ryan Singer about tourism and Native American culture on Route 66.

Tucumcari, NM

TEE PEE CURIO'

Route 66 put Native culture on the map. I mean, there's also plenty of co-opting Native culture to make money off of unenlightened tourists. It's kind of funny and kitschy, but it can also deter people from buying authentic Native art.

(Ryan is Navajo and an artist living in Albuquerque.)

I like to make fun of it all. I believe art can be a tool for that.

It is rainy and wet in Oklahoma, and my dedication to camping is wearing thin. In the drier states, I could bask in my (minimal) wilderness accomplishments.

Here, I am cold and wet and pooping in holes.

HOW to POOP in NATURE

① Dig a hole at least six inches deep and away from a water source.

② Poop in the hole.

③ Bury your poop.

Catoosa, OK

The Blue Whale of Catoosa is one of the quintessential roadside icons of Route 66.

It is a charming curiosity, a reminder of a time where safety rails were unheard of and a water slide was the pinnacle of summer fun.

You can climb into the Blue Whale's head, which is marked by graffiti by families and lovers.

inside!

It's not road trip season in Oklahoma,
and the gift shop and food stand are closed.

It is an unassuming park, and right now
it's completely empty and slightly damp.

Right now, in the early spring, it's a place for quiet thoughts for a girl and her dog.

In a sense, this deserted park encapsulates how I feel about the American Dream at the moment. I am both exhausted and eternally hopeful, skeptical that the American Dream still exists, and awed at the potential it still holds.

It's a treat to come across a store
advertising Route 66 cookies.

The store's proprietors, Charles Duboise
and his mother, are pretty enthusiastic
about both the cookies and the history
of Commerce, OK.

← ROUTE
66
sugar
cookie!

The Dairy King in Commerce used to be
a Marathon Gas Station in the Route 66
days. Now it serves ice cream, burgers,
and pretty good sugar cookies.

The Munger Moss Motel sign in Lebanon, MO

How do you feel about BBQ?

My good friend Leslie, from Los Angeles, is visiting her parents in Kansas City and invited me to stop by. Kansas City is two hours off my route, but I've been traveling alone for three weeks, and the promise of good company and delicious food is an easy choice.

Very positively, but after a nap.

133

I don't really have this kind of family village. The constant motion of a young immigrant-expat before the Facebook era is one where your best friends become beloved pen pals, and then distant friends, and then vague acquaintances, and then just curious strangers.

World's Largest Shuttlecocks, a sculpture at the Nelson-Atkins Museum of Art

I leave Kansas City with: a thorough education on the differences between Kansas City, MO, and Kansas City, KS, a fair amount of Civil War battleground facts, a ball for Bug, and an inexplicable longing for roots.

You can keep the ball, Bug.

I'll see ya back in LA!

Maybe I should stop pretending it's wanderlust when it is really just discontent. I've been wrapped up in trying to find something that feels like home instead of questioning why I even think that's so important.

Devil's Elbow, MO

ILLINOIS

By the time I enter Illinois, I've been sleeping in my car in the rain for several days.

Bug is in a great mood. I am not.

I try to be positive, but I'm craving the city. Chicago is calling to me as a beacon of hope, and by hope, I just mean the ability to order takeout from my phone.

Created by a fiberglass company, Muffler Men statues were deployed as advertising for roadside businesses across the United States in the '60s and '70s.

Many are now iconic statues that have been modified into unique and slightly disconcerting new shapes.

Chicken Boy is a modified Muffler Man in Highland Park, CA.

Route 66 has several of these Muffler Men statues.

I have obsessively visited them all.

a Paul Bunyan variant at Northern Arizona University in Flagstaff, AZ

Cozy Dog Drive In
Springfield, IL

← claims to be the home of the corndog.

147

I have a lot of thoughts in my head about immigrant America and the quiet coding of outsiderness, but right now I am just busy feeling grateful for the friendship and family offered to me.

Instead, I've come to feel more comfortable in motion. There is a calm in the unpredictability of road trip travel, of expecting long, empty roads and intentionally seeking out misadventures and beautiful strange detours.

Excited to head home?

Yeah, I think so.

Perhaps I've been overly preoccupied with the idea of home, of trying to force myself to be comfortable in a skin I've been trying to ease into for years—a skin finally labeled as both immigrant and American.

The traditional way to drive Route 66 is from east to west, mirroring the westward trail of people seeking a better life. In two more weeks, I'll be back in Los Angeles. It may not be home, but it is where I have a house, a partner, and friends. And I will stay and pause for a bit.

And then, perhaps, I'll just keep on going.

Okay, Bug-a-boo. Back on the road!

AN EPILOGUE

I drove Route 66 in April 2016, six months before Donald Trump would be elected President of the United States.

Since then, a lot of things have changed.

This comic feels like a record of a time when a brown girl could drive America fearlessly.

And I'm probably light enough to avoid trouble.

We're still gonna go, Bug. Can't let those jerks keep us down.